FRANCIS FRITH'S

HAILSHAM

PHOTOGRAPHIC MEMORIES

MARTIN ANDREW is an architectural and landscape historian, and a writer on outdoor matters; he is the Conservation Officer for Wycombe District Council in Buckinghamshire. He specialises in the landscape of lowland England, and combines his love of history, landscape and architecture in his writing. Since 1978 he has lived in Haddenham in Buckinghamshire with his wife and children. He is a keen long-distance walker and enjoys riding his classic motor cycle round the country lanes of the Chilterns. He was born in Doncaster, but spent most of his childhood in Ealing and Carshalton in Surrey. After university he worked for the Greater London Council's Historic Buildings Division, Buckinghamshire County Council and Salisbury District Council, before joining Wycombe District Council in 1990.

FRANCIS FRITH'S
PHOTOGRAPHIC MEMORIES

HAILSHAM

PHOTOGRAPHIC MEMORIES

MARTIN ANDREW

THE FRANCIS FRITH COLLECTION

First published in the United Kingdom in 2004 by
Frith Book Company Ltd

Limited Hardback Subscribers Edition Published in 2004
ISBN 1-85937-874-9

Paperback Edition 2004
ISBN 1-85937-875-7

British Library Cataloguing in Publication Data

Francis Frith's Hailsham - Photographic Memories
Martin Andrews

Frith Book Company Ltd
Frith's Barn, Teffont,
Salisbury, Wiltshire SP3 5QP
Tel: +44 (0) 1722 716 376
Email: info@francisfrith.co.uk
www.francisfrith.co.uk

Printed and bound in Great Britain

Front Cover: **HAILSHAM,** *High Street c1965* H6076
Frontispiece: **HAILSHAM,** *High Street 1900* 44955

*The colour-tinting is for illustrative purposes only, and is not
intended to be historically accurate*

AS WITH ANY HISTORICAL DATABASE THE FRITH ARCHIVE
IS CONSTANTLY BEING CORRECTED AND IMPROVED AND THE
PUBLISHERS WOULD WELCOME INFORMATION ON OMISSIONS
OR INACCURACIES

CONTENTS

FRANCIS FRITH
VICTORIAN PIONEER

FRANCIS FRITH, founder of the world-famous photographic archive, was a complex and multi-talented man. A devout Quaker and a highly successful Victorian businessman, he was philosophical by nature and pioneering in outlook.

By 1855 he had already established a wholesale grocery business in Liverpool, and sold it for the astonishing sum of £200,000, which is the equivalent today of over £15,000,000. Now a very rich man, he was able to indulge his passion for travel. As a child he had pored over travel books written by early explorers, and his fancy and imagination had been stirred by family holidays to the sublime mountain regions of Wales and Scotland. 'What lands of spirit-stirring and enriching scenes and places!' he had written. He was to return to these scenes of grandeur in later years to 'recapture the thousands of vivid and tender memories', but with a different purpose. Now in his thirties, and captivated by the new science of photography, Frith set out on a series of pioneering journeys up the Nile and to the Near East that occupied him from 1856 until 1860.

INTRIGUE AND EXPLORATION

These far-flung journeys were packed with intrigue and adventure. In his life story, written when he was sixty-three, Frith tells of being held captive by bandits, and of fighting 'an awful midnight battle to the very point of surrender with a deadly pack of hungry, wild dogs'. Wearing flowing Arab costume, Frith arrived at Akaba by camel sixty years before Lawrence of Arabia, where he encountered 'desert princes and rival sheikhs, blazing with jewel-hilted swords'.

He was the first photographer to venture beyond the sixth cataract of the Nile. Africa was still the mysterious 'Dark Continent', and Stanley and Livingstone's historic meeting was a decade into the future. The conditions for picture taking confound belief. He laboured for hours in his wicker dark-room in the sweltering heat of the desert, while the volatile chemicals fizzed dangerously in their trays. Back in London he exhibited his photographs and was 'rapturously cheered' by members of the Royal Society. His reputation as a photographer was made overnight.

VENTURE OF A LIFE-TIME

Characteristically, Frith quickly spotted the opportunity to create a new business as a specialist publisher of photographs. He lived in an era of immense and sometimes violent change.

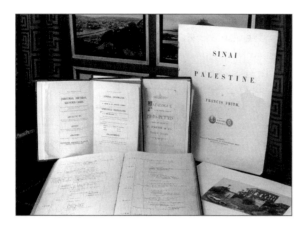

For the poor in the early part of Victoria's reign work was exhausting and the hours long, and people had precious little free time to enjoy themselves. Most had no transport other than a cart or gig at their disposal, and rarely travelled far beyond the boundaries of their own town or village. However, by the 1870s the railways had threaded their way across the country, and Bank Holidays and half-day Saturdays had been made obligatory by Act of Parliament. All of a sudden the working man and his family were able to enjoy days out and see a little more of the world.

With typical business acumen, Francis Frith foresaw that these new tourists would enjoy having souvenirs to commemorate their days out. In 1860 he married Mary Ann Rosling and set out on a new career: his aim was to photograph every city, town and village in Britain. For the next thirty years he travelled the country by train and by pony and trap, producing fine photographs of seaside resorts and beauty spots that were keenly bought by millions of Victorians. These prints were painstakingly pasted into family albums and pored over during the dark nights of winter, rekindling precious memories of summer excursions.

THE RISE OF FRITH & CO

Frith's studio was soon supplying retail shops all over the country. To meet the demand he gathered about him a small team of photographers, and published the work of independent artist-photographers of the calibre of Roger Fenton and Francis Bedford. In order to gain some understanding of the scale of Frith's business one only has to look at the catalogue issued by Frith & Co in 1886: it runs to some 670 pages, listing not only many thousands of views of the British Isles but also many photographs of most European countries, and China, Japan, the USA and Canada - note the sample page shown on page 9 from the hand-written Frith & Co ledgers recording the pictures. By 1890 Frith had created the greatest specialist photographic publishing company in the world, with over 2,000 sales outlets - more than the combined number that Boots and WH Smith have today! The picture on the next page shows the Frith & Co display board at Ingleton in the Yorkshire Dales (left of window). Beautifully constructed with a mahogany frame and gilt inserts, it could display up to a dozen local scenes.

POSTCARD BONANZA

The ever-popular holiday postcard we know today took many years to develop. In 1870 the Post Office issued the first plain cards, with a pre-printed stamp on one face. In 1894 they allowed other publishers' cards to be sent through the mail with an attached adhesive halfpenny stamp. Demand grew rapidly, and in 1895 a new size of postcard was permitted called the court card, but there was little room for illustration. In 1899, a year after Frith's death, a new card measuring 5.5 x 3.5 inches became the standard format, but it was not until 1902 that the divided back came into being, so that the address and message could be on one face and a full-size illustration on the other. Frith & Co were in the vanguard of postcard development: Frith's sons Eustace and Cyril continued their father's monumental task, expanding the number of views offered to the public and recording more and more places in Britain, as the

5	St Catherine's College	+		
6	Senate House & Library	+		
7			+	
8			+	
9	Gerrard Hostel Bridge	+	+	+ +
3 0	Geological Museum		+	
1	Addenbrookes Hospital		+	
2	St Mary's Church		+	
3	Fitzwilliam Museum, Pitt Press &c		+	
4			+	
5	Buxton, The Crescent		+	
6	The Colonnade		+	
7	Public Gardens		+	
8			+	
9	Haddon Hall, View from the Terrace		+	
4 0	Millers Dale		+	

coasts and countryside were opened up to mass travel.

Francis Frith had died in 1898 at his villa in Cannes, his great project still growing. The archive he created continued in business for another seventy years. By 1970 it contained over a third of a million pictures showing 7,000 British towns and villages.

FRANCIS FRITH'S LEGACY

Frith's legacy to us today is of immense significance and value, for the magnificent archive of evocative photographs he created provides a unique record of change in the cities, towns and villages throughout Britain over a century and more. Frith and his fellow studio photographers revisited locations many times down the years to update their views, compiling for us an enthralling and colourful pageant of British life and character.

We are fortunate that Frith was dedicated to recording the minutiae of everyday life. For it is this sheer wealth of visual data, the painstaking chronicle of changes in dress, transport, street layouts, buildings, housing, engineering and landscape that captivates us so much today. His remarkable images offer us a powerful link with the past and with the lives of our ancestors.

THE VALUE OF THE ARCHIVE TODAY

Computers have now made it possible for Frith's many thousands of images to be accessed almost instantly. Frith's images are increasingly used as visual resources, by social historians, by researchers into genealogy and ancestry, by architects and town planners, and by teachers involved in local history projects.

In addition, the archive offers every one of us an opportunity to examine the places where we and our families have lived and worked down the years. Highly successful in Frith's own era, the archive is now, a century and more on, entering a new phase of popularity. Historians consider the Francis Frith Collection to be of prime national importance. It is the only archive of its kind remaining in private ownership. Francis Frith's archive is now housed in an historic timber barn in the beautiful village of Teffont in Wiltshire. Its founder would not recognize the archive office as it is today. In place of the many thousands of dusty boxes containing glass plate negatives and an all-pervading odour of photographic chemicals, there are now ranks of computer screens. He would be amazed to watch his images travelling round the world at unimaginable speeds through internet lines.

The archive's future is both bright and exciting. Francis Frith, with his unshakeable belief in making photographs available to the greatest number of people, would undoubtedly approve of what is being done today with his lifetime's work. His photographs depicting our shared past are now bringing pleasure and enlightenment to millions around the world a century and more after his death.

HAILSHAM
AN INTRODUCTION

AUGUSTUS HARE, writing in 1894 in his well-known book *Sussex*, described Hailsham as 'a dreary little market town', noted perhaps unhappily for its rope factory, which 'had the privilege of supplying the cords used in prisons for executions'. In the latter fact Hare was correct, but in the former he was being somewhat harsh. Hailsham was always a small town, and only grew markedly after the railway arrived and the rope factories and breweries became larger in scale. Indeed, in the second half of the 19th century its cattle market was one of the largest and busiest in the county.

Much expansion in the 20th century saw Hailsham advancing to the north (swallowing up Upper Horsebridge in the process) and to the south, virtually to the edge of the Pevensey Levels. The modern town and its suburbs is shaped approximately like an hour-glass, with the core of the historic town just below the waist. The railway, the town's industrial artery, has gone, and is now a walking route, the Cuckoo Trail. Many of the older buildings have gone too, particularly on North Street and Western Road, but enough remains for us to pick out the history and evolution of this delightful small Sussex town.

The town grew slowly from medieval times to 1800, at which date the population was only about 900; the town at this time consisted of its market square and only two main streets, George Street and High Street, and a few back lanes. By 1861 the population had doubled to 2,098, and by the 1891 Census had risen further to 3,369, in the main owing to the

rope and twine manufacturing industries. During the 20th century the population grew to 12,775 by 1981, and is now about 14,000.

Hailsham is situated just above the 50-foot contour on the western edge of that great former sea marsh, the Pevensey Levels, which stretch eastward for about eight miles towards Bexhill. To the south a low ridge terminates at Pevensey; here there is a Roman fortress, and when William the Conqueror landed nearby in 1066, he converted it into a castle. In Roman times the Levels were part of the sea, but shingle banks cut it off from sea during Anglo-Saxon times and it became salt marshes - an Anglo-Saxon charter of 947 refers to 'fens' and 'marsh'. The lands in Hailsham held by Robert of Mortain at the time of *Domesday Book* (1087) included 17 salt pans. From about 1100 onwards, the Levels were gradually changed from salt marsh to reed beds and sedge meadows, and then to arable and pasture; this was largely as a result of the great Norman landowners undertaking reclamation on a grand scale. These included Gilbert, Earl of Pembroke and the Abbots of Battle. Although the salt pans had gone, the reeds and hemp grown on the Levels produced the raw materials for Hailsham's later wealth from the rope and twine industry.

Hailsham existed in Anglo-Saxon times, and the name means 'Haegel's settlement'. The name has been spelt differently over the centuries, assuming its present form in the 17th century; variations range from 'Eilesham' in *Domesday Book* to 'Elesham' in a source of 1523. It is also believed that the parish church was built on the site of an Anglo-Saxon hundred moot or local council meeting place, which was usually an earthen mound.

The next significant event in Hailsham's history was the granting of a weekly market by royal charter in 1252 to the new lord of the manor, Peter of Savoy, Earl of Richmond and uncle of Eleanor of Provence, Queen to Henry III. Peter had been granted Pevensey and much land in the area, including Hailsham, by the king in 1246. The market was held in the present Market Square, but presumably the burgage plots around the market place and along the High Street and George Street existed before this, so this charter may have recognised an already existing market - or perhaps an earlier charter does not survive. This seems likely, as there is a reference to a church here in 1229; also, although the church was rebuilt in the 15th century, there is one 13th-century carved capital which may have come from the earlier church (or perhaps from nearby Michelham Priory).

The market took place on Wednesdays, but it ceased in 1638 after nearly four centuries of existence. It was revived in 1786, but it changed its nature to become a leading cattle and livestock market during the 19th century. A brick market cross was demolished around 1800, presumably to make way for more stock space and to deal with a traffic obstruction. The cattle market prospered and outgrew Market Square; in 1862 it moved to a new three-acre site off Market Street. The present walls fronting Market Street were built in 1868.

Hailsham remained a small market town with minor craft industries such as rope-making and bell founding - the foundries are commemorated in the name Bell Banks Road. The church has a local cast bell dated 1665. The town remained small, serving its hinterland via its weekly market and tradesmen such as cobblers, braziers, saddle and harness makers and butchers. In the 1662 Hearth Tax returns there are about 70 houses listed; this is consistent with the size of the town, which by 1801 had increased to 132 houses and a population of 897.

Hailsham was therefore not a large place at this time; but there are quite a few buildings surviving or demolished in the 20th century that give or gave an idea of its Tudor and Stuart appearance, quite apart from the 15th-century parish church. These include the lost 15th-century timber-framed house at the junction of George and High Streets seen in views 48218 (page 20) and 44957 (page 35), and the surviving Fleur-de-Lys on the west side of Market Square, which was built about 1540 (view H6028a, page 32). Other losses include St Mary's on the east side of Market Square, which had a rear wing dated 1583 (demolished in 1937), and the original Crown Inn in George Street. This had a Tudor arch and fireplace which came to light when the Nat West demolished it in 1974; the building had been an inn since well before a bequest in 1632. Survivors of note include The Stone, a 14th-century Wealden house in Vicarage Lane, and further north the 15th-century timber-framed Old Thatched Cottage in Hempstead Lane (view H6066 on page 49). During the 18th century, Georgian fronts and new houses arrived: the best two are the Manor House in Market Street, dated 1740, and the Vicarage in Vicarage Lane (view 44962, page 16), also earlier 18th-century. Other examples are the Georgian front added to the George Inn, and New House of 1783 in George Street, later Courtlandts (views 48221s and H6028b, both on page 39).

In the late 18th century Hailsham was stirred from its agrarian slumbers by having a barracks built in the 1780s, and also by a number of energetic men. These entrepreneurs transformed the town into a centre for rope making (and brewing – see below). One was Thomas Burfield, who arrived in Hailsham around 1780 as an itinerant saddler and horse-collar maker. He started a saddlery business in the High Street in 1807, and soon diversified into rope, twine and string making, building factories in South Road. These incorporated immensely long rope walks where the hemp was twisted into ropes. Besides Burfield & Sons, many other rope walks and rope works were established, including Green Brothers on Summerheath Road. Other works were situated behind the Crown and 89 South Street, in Stoney Lane, in Mill Road, in Bell Banks and in Common Road. By the 1880s, Burfield & Sons and Green Brothers (founded by George Green, a yarn spinner at Burfields who set up on his own) each employed over 200 hands. Greens made official hangmen's ropes. All the rope works diversified into similar related products such as hop pockets, sacking, mill sails and whipcord, while in World War II Green Brothers made camouflage netting, sails, hangar covers, and even 500 dummy aircraft to confuse German air reconnaissance.

Hailsham was thus famous in the 19th century for its rope and twine manufacturing, and its growth was undoubtedly helped by the arrival of the railway as a branch line from Polegate, which opened in May 1849. The station was near the junction of South Road and George Street, and the fact that it was a terminus was marked by the name Terminus Place. The railway did not continue north until 1880 when the connection to Eridge was opened, but by then Hailsham's pattern of expansion was set. A second factor that helped the town grow to meet the labour demands of its industries and trades was the enclosure of Hailsham Common to the south and west of the town in 1855. New houses and terraces were developed, ranging from artisan terraces to middle-class villas to service both the labourers, the skilled workers and the new middle classes of the expanding town. Much of the terrace and smaller housing survives today, but it is ironic that the streets of villas such as North Road suffered worst in the redevelopment in the second half of the 20th-century.

Rope making was the major industry, supplemented by the manufacture of the traditional Sussex trug basket (now made only in and around Herstmonceux) and other smaller industries. The town also had a commercial brewery, which was

opened in 1827 by Thomas Gooch who came to Hailsham from Norwich. It was built in Battle Road, at one time called Brewery Road. New buildings were erected in 1887, but the brewery closed; the 1887 building became for a while a Roman Catholic church, and is now occupied by a motor accessory manufacturer. The rope works have also gone. Burfield & Sons' factories on South Road are perpetuated in the name Burfield Park Industrial Estate, and Green Brothers' Summerheath Road factory in the names of closes of modern houses, Rope Walk and Green Grove.

The enclosure of the common in 1855 was complete except for the Common Pond, which was retained by Lord Sackville. Originally dammed as a carp pond to the manor house, the pond is an ancient one. There is a reference to it in the Sussex Assize Roll (the county court records) for 1263, when Gilbert, son of Gilbert Godseb, drowned while bathing in the pond. By 1922, when Lord Sackville sold the pond to the Parish Council for £3,000, the town had expanded onto the enclosed common to its north and west, and Bell Banks Road was firmly within the town. To its west is the road renamed Station Road in honour of the new 1849 rail line, which ran parallel to the road. The railway is nowadays a somewhat distant memory – it was closed in 1968, and its tracks were lifted and the station demolished. You can follow its route through cuttings, across embankments and through the countryside as the Cuckoo Trail: this extends from Polegate, three miles to the south of Hailsham, through the heart of Hailsham, mostly in a cutting, and all the way to Heathfield via Horam, where the Express Dairy depot provided much of the railway's regular freight traffic.

During the later 19th century Hailsham steadily acquired the appurtenances of Victorian township. The new combined police superintendent's office, house and courthouse at the north end of the High Street was built in 1861 to replace the old one further down the High Street. The superintendent had under him a force of one sergeant and twelve constables (considerably more than in 2004). The Board School was opened in 1878 in Battle Road. Gas arrived to light the streets and heat and light the town's houses - the coke was processed at the gas works; and the town received a recreation ground, formerly part of the common, on Western Road in 1885. A Parish Council took over the administration of the town in1895.

The 20th century saw continued expansion and improvement in the town. Commerce in the shape of new bank branches arrived, sweeping some older building into oblivion: the London and County on the east side of Market Square arrived in 1909, and the Westminster Bank (at the corner of High Street and George Street on the north-west corner of Market Square) replaced a fine 15th-century timber-framed building by an anaemic Jacobethan effort in 1930. Other buildings went too. St Mary's, a good early Georgian front on the east side of Market Square with an older 1583 rear wing disappeared in 1937, and the Hailsham Pavilion cinema in George Street replaced an older building in 1921. In the High Street many buildings were replaced by others, including in around 1960 the present Woolworth's; during that decade in particular the old shop fronts mostly went in favour of ill-conceived modern ones. The centre of the High Street opposite Vicarage Fields saw several old buildings demolished and replaced by the Quintins shopping centre in the 1980s. Vicarage Fields, originally called Parsonage Fields,

were themselves built over by another shopping precinct (of no architectural distinction, although not actively unpleasant) between 1965 and 1968.

As we have seen, the railway went in 1968, and the area west of the High Street along North Street and Western Road was comprehensively redeveloped and most earlier buildings replaced. Factories such as Green Brothers on Summerheath Road were replaced by housing. Much of this change was inevitable. The town is certainly vibrant and popular today, and its streets and shopping precincts are packed on a Saturday. It is a relaxed and pleasant town, and obviously popular with its inhabitants and visitors from surrounding villages. It retains sufficient historic character to maintain its distinctiveness - it is certainly infinitely more attractive than Polegate, for example. It is surrounded by varied and attractive countryside, from the South Downs and the Weald and the meandering Cuckmere River valley to the vast flat lands of the Pevensey Levels, these last for so many years of Hailsham's history a key to its economic activity.

This collection of views covers some sixty-five years of the town's history, and shows it before the major changes that arrived in the 1960s. It is a fascinating record of Hailsham, and the nearby villages and countryside are covered in the two last chapters. I really greatly enjoyed visiting this former rope making town again after an interval of about three years. I hope you enjoy the views selected for this book as much.

HAILSHAM: ST MARY'S PARISH CHURCH AND OTHER CHURCHES

THE CHURCH AND THE VICARAGE
1900 44962

The first chapter starts in the heart of the market town of Hailsham with this deceptively rural view of the parish church, with the fine 18th-century vicarage to the right. This view was taken from a pond on the south side of Vicarage Road; while the pond survives today, its margins are more tidy and less picturesque, with a chain link fence to the lane at the right. The vicarage has a good slated mansard roof and ornate dormers.

► **THE CHURCH**
From the South East 1900 44963

One of the earliest references to the church in Hailsham is in 1229, some thirty years before Henry II granted the already existing town a market charter. However, the town was served originally by a chapel-of-ease from Hellingly parish, which may explain why Hailsham's church is built behind the High Street rather than within it. This view, from the south east near Vicarage Road, shows a heavily Victorianised medieval church; it further suffered in 1943 when a bomb blast destroyed all its stained glass.

◄ **THE CHURCH**
The Interior 1900
44964

This interior view of the church shows the 15th-century nave arcades and chancel arch; the ghost of the original roof line can be seen high above the chancel arch. The medieval roof survives, but it was lifted in 1889 when the Victorian clerestory was added. The Victorian improving biblical text over the chancel arch has been replaced by the more familiar 'Jesus said: I am the way, the truth and the life'.

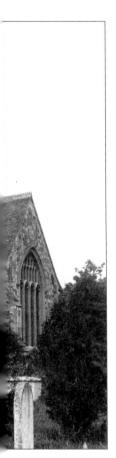

▲ **ST MARY'S CHURCH,** *From the South c1955* H6031

This view is taken from the brick four-centred arch into Market Square. The brick footpath heads towards the porch which, with the south aisle, was added in 1870 to designs by H E Rumble. Above are the round quatrefoil windows of the clerestory added in 1889, which must have made the interior much lighter. On the left are the backs of buildings that front the High Street, while the yews and hollies in this view survive today.

◀ **THE CHURCH**
Looking North West c1965
H6086

Another view, similar to H6031 (above), shows the brick-paved path and the holly bushes. At the left is a silver birch, which also survives today. The fine 15th-century tower with its Victorian pinnacles is built in local Wealden sandstone; its walls are the least renewed or refaced part of the church, whose three Victorian restorations in 1870, 1878 and 1889 transformed the appearance of the medieval church's nave and chancel – indeed, the chancel was entirely rebuilt.

▼ ST MARY'S CHURCH, *The West Tower c1955* H6030

This last view of St Mary's Church gives a clearer impression of the relatively unrestored tower stonework. The tower contains a bell cast in the local bell foundries in 1665; the location of these foundries is commemorated in the name Bell Banks Road, a road to the south that runs from Market Street to the ponds. Out to the left is the Vicarage Field shopping mall, while beyond the silver birch is the church hall extension opened in 1985.

► THE CHURCH
The Queen Victoria Memorial Gates 1902
48222s

When Austin's gun shop burned down in June 1894, it gave the church an opportunity to gain direct access to the High Street. In the event the land was bought by the Parish Council in 1898, and the stone piers and gates were opened in December 1901 as a memorial to Queen Victoria, who had died the preceding January. The church thus gained its extra access from the town centre.

◀ **THE BAPTIST CHURCH,** *Market Street 1900* 44965

This chapter finishes with two views of non-conformist churches as a counterpoint to the parish church. The first is down Market Street. The Baptist church was built early in the19th century; it was attached to a farmhouse, the tile-hung building to the right. Soon after this view was taken, the church was virtually rebuilt in 1905, reopening in 1910 after 'extensive repairs and alterations'. The tile-hung wing to the right survived unchanged, but the church was clad in brick with stone dressings to the windows. The trees have gone, and the field to the right is now occupied by 1970s houses, Southerden Close.

▶ **THE WESLEYAN CHURCH** *1902* 48223

At the opposite end of the High Street, past the North Street junction, stands the Wesleyan church; its foundation stone was laid by the splendidly named Williamson Lamplouch in September 1868. To the left, the bell turret belongs to the Old Court House and former police station, built a little earlier in 1861. The late 20th century has done its worst and replaced the church's windows by plastic ones and roughcast-coated the smooth render. The railings and walls have gone, and a modernistic and an inappropriate 1960s wing-roofed porch has been added.

HAILSHAM: THE HIGH STREET, MARKET SQUARE AND GEORGE STREET

HIGH STREET
From Market Square 1902   48218

The second chapter visits the main street of the old market town, starting in Market Square looking into the High Street. To the right is the brick archway into the churchyard, but the buildings on the right have gone. Apart from the timber-framed building on the left corner, the start of George Street, most of the rest remain. The Good Intent pub to the left of the churchyard archway is now the Homely Maid tea rooms.

21

HIGH STREET
1902 48483

This view, clearer than the similar 44954s (page 21), shows the elegant gas lamp to the newsagent and tobacconist (left). Parker's beyond is mainly timber-framed - the framing is now visible from the north. To the right the ivy-clad house is now a shop, Tendring Garden, and of course now without the railings. Beyond is the edge of the former Parsonage Field, its horse chestnut-lined fence providing welcome shade on a hot summer's day; it is now the site of Vicarage Fields shopping precinct, which opened in 1968.

HIGH STREET

c1965 H6076

For this 1960s view, Frith's photographer is looking north from the upper floor of the quite new Woolworth's towards the horse chestnut trees edging Parsonage Field - they screen the Comrades Club seen in view H6049 (page 26). The trees have now gone, and the Vicarage Fields shopping precinct opens up the streetscape. The Boots shop (this side of the trees) is now the Tendring Garden, a florist's and gardening shop, and Cruttendens, the radio and TV shop (right), is still in that line as Clear View, a TV and rental shop.

HIGH STREET

c1955   H6028c

This view looks southwards past the News Store to the Crown Hotel, now renamed the Corn Exchange. Beyond, the building that is set forward (extreme left) went not long after this view was taken, to be replaced by a two-storey flat-roofed Woolworth's store. To the far right, the building that was a house in previous views has become two shops: now it is one, a Costcutter shop.

HIGH STREET, *The Comrades Club and the War Memorial c1955*   H6049

Just to the left of Tendring Garden is the war memorial, erected at the edge of Parsonage Field and unveiled in November 1920. Beyond is the British Legion Comrades Club, which opened soon after in the mid 1920s. It was replaced by the Hailsham Club nearer the church in order to make way for the Vicarage Fields shopping precinct, which was started in 1965 and opened in 1968. The war memorial is now in a low walled area as part of the precinct's hard landscaping.

HIGH STREET NEWS STORE
Detail taken from 48483

THOMAS WHITE, THE GROCER'S
Detail taken from 44957

CRUTTENDENS, HIGH STREET
Detail taken from H6076

CYCLISTS REST, MARKET SQUARE
Detail taken from 44952

HIGH STREET
1902   48485

We have moved north past the two shopping precincts. An alley to the left leads to North Street. Behind the tall tree on the left was the Infant School, opened in 1862 and enlarged in 1882, now a carpet warehouse. The long stucco-fronted building on the right is now barely recognisable, for its ground floor is now entirely occupied by modern shop fronts. Indeed, all the other shop fronts in this view have long been replaced by less attractive ones. However, elements of the calico warehouse shop front survive (left); the shop is now Wards menswear and dress-hire.

HIGH STREET
1900   44955

Now past the North Street junction, Frith's photographer is looking north past the covered wagon with its load of barrels and sacks towards the pedimented gable of the 1868 Wesleyan church on the right; the police station and court house of 1861 are beyond. All the buildings in this view survive, although the shop fronts have been renewed, while the building on the left is boarded up and looking sorry for itself (January 2004).

MARKET SQUARE
Looking South 1902
48219s

Back at the south end of the High Street, Frith's photographer is looking south-west towards White & Sons, the grocers, who first traded on this site on the corner of George Street in 1816. There used to be a brick-built market cross here, but it was removed around 1800 as a hazard to traffic. The cattle market itself moved down Market Street to a new off-road site in 1862.

MARKET SQUARE, *Old Houses c1955*   H6028a

Fleur-de-Lys, the timber-framed building, is one of Hailsham's most interesting and oldest buildings. Now the town council offices, it dates from around 1540; it has had a number of previous uses, including being the town Poor House (from 1762 to 1854), then a post office, an undertaker's and a wheelwright's. In 1889 the left part was burnt down and replaced by the gable-fronted fire station, which is now a kebab restaurant.

MARKET SQUARE
Looking South East down Market Street 1900   44952

Frith's late Victorian photographer is now looking from Market
Square south east into Market Street, with the ornamented 1868
walls of the 1862 relocated cattle market beyond the tall, bare tree.
The gabled roof to the right is the fire station of 1889, which we also
see in view H6028a (page 32). The Georgian house on the left was
on the corner of Vicarage Road, then a narrow lane, and was
demolished in 1937 for junction improvement and road widening.
It had a rear wing dated 1583. Beyond, the photographer's house
went in around 1905 for a Barclays Bank.

MARKET SQUARE
Looking West into George Street 1899   44957

On the left is Thomas White, the grocer's established here in 1816; the premises are now The Link Coffee Shop, a Christian bookshop and coffee bar. The 15th-century timber-framed and jettied house on the right was replaced by a Jacobethan-style Westminster Bank in 1930 (see view H6028e, page 36). The building to its left, W Ellis's china shop, was demolished in 1974 for an extension to the bank, now Nat West. A Tudor archway and fireplace were uncovered during the tragic demolition.

GEORGE STREET *c1955* H6028e

This 1950s view looks along George Street from the junction with the High Street. On the right is the 1930 rebuilt bank; the plaque over the door is inscribed 'Aedificata Circa MDL', ('built about 1550'), referring to the Tudor building this one so unnecessarily replaced, and 'Restituta MCMXXX' ('rebuilt 1930'), although other sources date the rebuild at 1935. The ornate gabled stucco building on the right in the middle distance is the facade of the Hailsham Pavilion, built as a cinema and opened in 1921. It became a bingo hall in 1967, and in 2000 an arts centre, The Pavilion.

▶ **GEORGE STREET**
The George Hotel 1900
44958x

Now in George Street, the camera is looking towards Market Square with the George Hotel on the right. Beyond is the tile-hung gable of The Link coffee shop. The George has a Georgian 18th-century front, but there are older parts inside. Until the Courthouse and police station were built at the north end of the High Street in 1861 the petty sessions were held in two upstairs rooms at the George. The information-covered flat-roofed structure has now gone, and the pub is under an apparently much-needed full-scale repair (January 2004).

GEORGE STREET *1900*   44958c

The north side of the street has seen some changes since 1900, most notably the demolition of the chequer-brick building beyond the Golden Boot, William Stanford's public house (note the gilded boot sign by the fascia) to make way for the ornate classical-fronted Pavilion Cinema which opened in 1921. The building to the left of it survives as a takeaway restaurant, Padlers, and the 18th-century stucco house with the columned doorcase and bay window, Roseneath, now has shop fronts and is also a restaurant, in this case a Chinese one.

▶ **GEORGE STREET**
1902 48486s

We have moved a little further west from 44958c (page 37). The house on the left now has a shop front, and is a hairdresser's. The George stands on the right in the middle distance. Facing the camera at the far end are two houses on the east side of Market Square: the left-hand pale stucco-fronted one was replaced by a brick bank, the London and County Bank, in 1909, and the right-hand one, St Mary's, went in 1937.

◀ **GEORGE STREET**
Downford House 1902
48489s

At the west end of George Street there were a number of villas (the most notable is Courtlandts, which stands to the left of Downford House). This stucco-fronted villa was built in 1838; Downford House now has a less sylvan garden, and the railings and upper parts of the gate piers have gone. It is now offices. The noted architectural historian and historian of Sussex, L F Salzman (1878-1971), spent much of his early life in this house.

▲ **GEORGE STREET,** *Courtlandts 1902* 48221s

Next to Downford House stands Courtlandts, built in 1793 as New House for a John Bristow. During the Napoleonic Wars, Hailsham acquired a new barracks, built in 1803, and the house was occupied by the Barrack Master, Major Philip van Cortlandt, hence its later name. He was an American Loyalist and a descendant of the Dutch founder of New York. Loyalists were those very numerous Americans who supported Britain in the American War of Independence.

◀**GEORGE STREET,** *Courtlandts c1955* H6028b

The centre part of the house is Georgian. The bay-windowed wings were added by William Strickland, who had bought the house in 1881 (the left-hand one after 1902, as it does not appear in the 1902 photograph, No 48221s, above). A rear wing is dated 1875. In 1932 the house was bought by Hailsham Rural District Council for its own use, but it was sold in 1982 and is now offices.

HAILSHAM: AROUND THE TOWN

A VIEW FROM THE SOUTH *1902* 48482s

The third chapter's tour moves a little further afield within Hailsham. The town's expansion began with the arrival of the railway in 1849, when large numbers of terraced houses and villas were built to accommodate the growing population of this successful rope and twine-making town. This Edwardian view looks northwards towards the town from a hay-making field, with new and recently built houses in the middle distance.

41

▶ NORTH STREET
1900 44959s

Just past Courtlandts, North Street curves northwards to join the far end of the High Street. North Street was lined by mid and late Victorian villas, and was one of the best addresses in the town. However, this view is mightily changed now: the three right-hand villas have been replaced by the car park and shops of the Quintins, a shopping precinct centred on a Co-op supermarket. The buildings in the far distance survive, but North Street is now merely an inner relief road by-passing the High Street, which is now one-way (north to south).

WESTERN ROAD
1900 44960

The railway originally ended at Terminus Place (which is hardly surprising), and housing was laid out along the old lane onto the common: this became Western Road, with Summer Heath Road a turning off in the distance of this view. All the houses on the right, apart from the one in the middle distance with two hipped-roofed bay windows, have since been demolished. The 1960s library, together with modern housing estates, have replaced them. The survivor is now a Citizens Advice Bureau and a working men's club. The recreation ground is on the left.

◄ WESTERN ROAD
The Recreation Ground
c1965 H6088

On the south side of Western Road is the Recreation Ground; it was enclosed in 1885, having formerly been part of Hailsham common. In this view the road is off to the right out of shot. The verandahed building is the pavilion, which opened in 1909 and cost £300 to build. It has since been refurbished with a coated metal roof resembling pantiles.

WESTERN ROAD
The Cricket Field
c1955 H6052

The second view in the Recreation Ground was taken to the south of the pavilion beside one of the trees seen in view H6088 on page 43; to its left, a boy is watching a game of cricket. The houses beyond are on South Road, another road developed in later Victorian times near the railway station. Cricket had long been played on the common: the earliest recorded game took place in 1788 between the Gentlemen of Hailsham and the Gentlemen of Herstmonceux. The cricket club itself has continuous records from 1884.

▶ **BELL BANKS ROAD**
The Pond c1955
H6055

The name of this road commemorates the local bell-founding industry which was based in bell pits and foundries along this lane – indeed, the parish church has a 17th-century tenor bell cast in Bell Bank. Bell Banks Road is to the left of this view, with the houses of a 1950s council estate on the right. No 2 Archers Walk faces the camera. Out of view to the left is Station Road; it leads uphill to Terminus Place, where until 1880 the railway did indeed terminate.

BELL BANKS ROAD
The Pond c1955 H6056

This pond with its island is a most attractive feature in the outer part of the town. While it is somewhat municipalised nowadays, it is very ancient. The earliest reference to it is a sad one in 1263, in the Sussex Assize Roll for that year. It is reported to the coroner that one Gilbert, son of Gilbert Godseb, drowned in the pond while bathing. The walled enclosure on the far bank is inscribed 'This Sheltered Corner was Endowed by Harold and Winifred Morgan in Memory of their Father, James Henry Morgan'.

◀ **BELL BANKS ROAD**
The Common, the Pond c1955 H6097

The commons were largely enclosed in 1855, but the pond area was retained by the lord of the manor, Lord Sackville. It was finally bought by the council in 1922 for £3,000, and became a public open space. A popular location, it is somewhat surrounded by uninspiring housing estates and housing, such as the 1950s Bell Banks bungalows opposite, but it and Bell Banks Road are living links with the town's distant past.

ERSHAM ROAD
c1960 H6065

Ersham Road to the south of the town centre is typical of the relatively modern expansion of the town. Ersham Lodge was a Victorian house in substantial grounds which was demolished around 1930, and its land was developed for housing as Ersham Park: Windsor Road, The Avenue, Park Close and Ersham Way. On the left are 1950s bungalows, and behind the pedestrian (right) is the turning into Windsor Road and Ersham Way. The houses hidden by hedges along this stretch are Edwardian, with the 1930s estate behind them.

THE BOARD SCHOOL 1900   44966s

The last three views are found to the north of the High Street. The first is in Battle Road, a right turn where the High Street becomes London Road. This building is the Board School, which was formally opened in September 1878 with Charles Towler as its first headmaster; the Hailsham School Board had been set up after the 1870 Education Act. Much extended in both directions in the 1960s and 1970s, it is now thriving as Hailsham Community College.

▲ HEMPTSTEAD LANE
The Old Thatched Cottage c1960 H6066

The last two views in Hailsham itself are of a timber-framed cottage on Hempstead Lane, once in the countryside but now firmly within the town's 20th-century expansion - this sweeps past the lane northward for a further half mile to Upper Horsebridge and the A271. Along Hempstead Lane were scattered farmhouses and cottages, each with its own well; at the east end, at Leap Cross, were grazing commons. What is now Numbers 1 and 2 is the easternmost of these cottages, a survivor from those times.

◄ HEMPTSTEAD LANE
The Thatched Cottage c1965 H6090

The road junction immediately east of the cottage is Leap Cross, first recorded in the 15th century; the name 'lep' or 'lepe' refers to a medieval custom allowing tenants to graze the commons between Michaelmas (September 29) and Martinmas (11 November). The thatched and timber-framed 15th-century house was originally built as a single yeoman's farmhouse. Later it was subdivided into two and given lean-to stores at each end.

MAGHAM DOWN
The Old Forge Guest House c1960 M274004

At the junction of Old Road and the main road, the A271, was this entrepreneurial former village smithy. Like many blacksmiths, the owner diversified into car repairs and petrol sales after World War I - the former smithy, adapted to its new use, is the single-storey building. By the 1950s it had also become a guesthouse and tea room (right), and by 2004 the garage element had gone, and it is now a hotel and guesthouse.

A TOUR EAST OF HAILSHAM

MAGHAM DOWN
*The Red Lion and Post Office
c1955*   M274003

Our first rural tour heads eastwards, skirting to the north of the Pevensey Levels, those great marshes largely drained during the Middle Ages, and following the road that heads for Ninfield and Bexhill. Magham Down, about two miles north east of Hailsham, is where the road rises onto the higher ground it follows towards Bexhill. The late Victorian Red Lion pub on the left is closed and for sale (January 2004), while the post office on the right is, as in many other villages, closed and now a house, Post Office House.

MAGHAM DOWN
Old Road c1955   M274005

Old Road heads north east, and runs parallel to the main road. This view looks back towards the Old Forge Guest House in the distance. This lane has been more heavily developed since the 1950s, but it retains its rural character. In the right foreground is the turning into Squab Lane. Magham is first recorded in a document of 1261, but the name is Anglo-Saxon, meaning 'settlement of Maecga'. Maecga was obviously a war-band leader, as his name is Old English for 'warrior'.

HERSTMONCEUX
The Castle, the West Front 1890 25345

A mile south of the main road, on a spur some 80 feet high on the edge of the Pevensey Levels, lies the parish church of Herstmonceux and this spectacular brick-built castle. This 1890 view shows it well before its careful restoration; this started in 1911 under Colonel Claude Lowther, but was completed by Sir Paul Latham MP in 1932. Licence to crenellate (to build a castle) was granted by Henry VI in 1440 to Sir Roger Fiennes, Treasurer of the King's Household.

▶ **HERSTMONCEUX**
The Castle, the Inner Courtyard 1890 25349

Sir Roger Fiennes' ancestor, Sir John, had married the heiress Maud de Monceux in 1320, the last of the family that had held the manor since the 12th century and had given the village the second part of its name; the other part, 'hyrst', is Anglo-Saxon for 'a wooded hill'. This view within the courtyard of the castle shows it after the 1770s stripping out to a hollow shell for the building of Herstmonceux Place, a house designed by Samuel Wyatt. Nowadays, in its restored state the castle is an international study centre affiliated with the University of Kingston, Ontario, in Canada. Before this, it had been the site of the Greenwich Royal Observatory (from 1957 to 1979), and the observatory buildings are now a public museum, the Herstmonceux Science Centre.

◀ **HERSTMONCEUX**
The Parish Church c1950
H328013

All Saints' Church looks out over the marshes by Church Farm, and stands at the west gates to the castle (not now the public entrance, which is from the Wartling Road). Its square tower with an oak-shingled spire is of about 1190. Much of the church is rendered, with the chancel and east chapel in 15th-century Flemish brick, probably built at the same time as the castle itself. Indeed, inside are monuments to the Fiennes family. The main village migrated or grew up along the main Bexhill-Hailsham road over a mile away, giving the church the feel of being the lord of the manor's private chapel.

▲ **HERSTMONCEUX,** *Hailsham Road c1965* H328023

Back on the main road, this is the real centre of the modern village; there is a good range of shops and pubs, and the school, Herstmonceux Church of England Primary School, lies behind the fence on the right, a late Victorian building with 1960s additions. On the left, at the corner of West End, is the Woolpack Inn, which still has the corrugated iron clad function room we see in this view. The garage next door, though, has closed, and is now a pine furniture shop.

◀ **HERSTMONCEUX**
Gardner Street c1965
H328025

Round the bend, past the old garage, the A271 continues as Gardner Street, the main shopping street of the village. On the left, the weatherboarded bank has been demolished and replaced by a car business, but the store beyond remains as a general store and post office. On the right, the bay window beyond the Austin A30 is still W J Crouch, the family butcher. In the distance is Higham Farm, with its barns now converted to dwellings.

▼ **WINDMILL HILL,** *The Windmill c1955* W448305

Continuing eastwards, the A271 passes through the hamlet of Windmill Hill at the eastern end of Herstmonceux parish where the land rises to over 180 feet. It was here that the village's windmill was built on a knoll. It was a post mill, and by the 1950s was in a poor state and without its sails. Today (January 2004) it is under restoration and scaffolded and sheeted. In fact, only the base and the main central post are in place.

► **WINDMILL HILL**
Old Cottages c1955
W448003

The hamlet contains some older cottages, and we can see some of them in this view looking west: they include the tile-hung Elm Cottages and the painted weatherboarded Field House to their right. Beyond is a pair of Victorian gabled cottages, once a shop but now a house, The Gables. Note the iron lattice-work electricity poles on the left. The road has since the 1950s been widened to take in the grass verge.

◄ **WINDMILL HILL**
Posey Green c1955
W448002

We are now looking east. The road widens to form Posey Green, with the 1930s Horseshoe Inn on the right out of camera shot; it is a rambling mix of local sandstone and timber-framing with a huge horseshoe-arched porch entry. The village hall on the right has given way to houses, but the cottages on the left remain. The No 15 bus to Bexhill (centre) has stopped beside the white-painted Windmill Hill Store and a garage, whose petrol pumps can just be seen.

▶ **BOREHAM STREET**
The White Friars Hotel c1955
B645011

Wartling is another parish like Herstmonceux, with its parish church and part of the village over a mile south of the main road and on the edge of the Pevensey Levels. The main settlement along the main road is called Boreham Street. It is an attractive village, and at the west end, on the corner of Wood Lane, is the White Friars Hotel; we see it here from Wood Lane, with the main road passing between the creeper-clad hotel and the rendered house. Currently (January 2004) under restoration and hidden behind scaffolding and sheeting, the building has 16th-century origins.

PEVENSEY
The Castle from the South West 1890 25334

From Boreham Street we head south through Wartling and out across the flatland of the Pevensey Levels to Pevensey itself, which stands on its low ridge or island amid the former marshes. It was here in the 4th century AD that the Romans built Anderida, one of their chain of Saxon Shore forts intended to defend the Roman province of Britannia from Saxon raiders. Much later, William the Conqueror arrived in 1066, and soon after a castle was built within the Roman walls. These still survive, and so does much of the castle. This view looks through the ruins of the 13th-century gatehouse.

PEVENSEY, *The Castle 1894* 34480

In Roman and medieval times the castle was on the sea, but this has retreated half a mile away. This view shows the 13th-century drum towers of the castle and the wet moat, now protected by a rustic fence. The ivy has gone; this important medieval castle and Roman fortress ruins were properly consolidated after the Duke of Devonshire gave it to the nation in 1925, some years after these two views were taken. There is now a bridge over the moat beyond the far tower.

PEVENSEY, *The School from the Footbridge c1955* P50043

Captioned by Frith in the 1950s 'A Pretty Spot', this view looks north across a footbridge over a stream towards the eastern end of the village. In the distance is the ornamental gable of the village school built in 1876, now a house called, unsurprisingly, The Old School House. The middle ground is now less rural, with fences either side of the path; to the right are 1960s elderly persons' bungalows, St Nicholas Close. In the far distance is the line of the High Street.

WILLINGDON, *The Windmill c1955*   W446330

Just south of Polegate, on the A22, is Willingdon Windmill. This tower mill dates from1817; it was restored in the 1980s by the Eastbourne and District Preservation Society (there are tie-rod plaques dated 1989), and it is sometimes open to the public. To the right are 1950s council houses behind neat hedges. The high hedge in front of the mill encloses a small field - the hedge today is lower and trimmer. In the distance there are now 1960s estate houses.

WILLINGDON
The View from the Downs c1965 W446334

Now south of the windmill and climbing onto the South Downs, Frith's photographer looks west to Willingdon village below; the road on the right is Tas Combe Way with its trees and spacious verges. Indeed, this view looks from Butt's Brow into Tas Combe below the grassy foreground which gave the road its name. Beyond are the housing estates of Lower Willingdon and Hampden Park, all now much expanded.

POLEGATE, *The Level Crossing c1960*   P259027

Polegate barely existed until the railway arrived in 1846; initially it was the station for Eastbourne, connected to it by a horse omnibus. A branch line soon followed, and Eastbourne station opened in 1849, but Polegate grew, and until it was by-passed recently it was something of a bottleneck on the Bexhill Road, the A27. The station, to the left out of shot, is a modern rebuild, but the Victorian signal cabin on the right survives, and still controls the busy level crossing.

61

POLEGATE, *The High Street looking North c1965* P259026

We are looking north from the railway station and level crossing, and there is little of distinction in the architecture. An 1870s terrace of yellow brick flats over shops runs south from the scaffolding on the left, but the rest is mediocre 1930s and 1950s suburban building, apart from the Polegate Inn on the right (a Victorian inn, bizarrely renamed the Dinkum) and a United Reformed church of about 1900 in the left middle distance.

POLEGATE
The High Street looking South c1965 P259024

As we look south from just across the railway, things improve. There are 1890s brick cottages on the left, and beyond the turning into St John's Road are mostly Victorian villas. Beyond that is the well treed churchyard of the parish church with its broach spire, built in 1874-76 after Polegate became a separate parish. On the right Elizabeth Court, two blocks of six flats, lie beyond unpleasant early 1960s flats over shops complete with flat roofs and pointed tile hanging.

POLEGATE, *The Horse and Groom c1955* P259014

Our last view in this chapter before turning north back to Hailsham shows the Horse and Groom pub at the junction of the High Street and the Eastbourne Road, the A22. Something of a road-house in 1920s Sussex vernacular style in timber-framing, brick and stone, it is a landmark along a dull suburban main road. In the aprons of the first floor bay windows are rather good plaster reliefs of a horse being led by a groom. Apart from a larger car park and shortened chimney stacks, little has changed in this view since the 1950s.

A TOUR WEST OF HAILSHAM

HORAM, *The Village c1960*   H329029

The fifth chapter's tour initially heads about five miles north of Hailsham to Horam, a scattered hamlet until the railway arrived in 1880. A major Express Dairies depot grew up here, with the railway playing a key part and the dairy providing most of its goods traffic. Until the 18th century the area had been an important centre for the Sussex iron industry - the cannon on the inn sign of the Horam Inn is a reminder of this (left). The station, closed in the 1960s, was down the road to the left, and the 1890s shops were built not long after the station opened. On the right behind the trees is the famous Merrydown Cider factory.

HORAM, *The Parish Church c1955*   H329024

The parish church is on Horebeech Lane, a turning a little to the south of the shops in view H329029 (on pages 64-65), and dates from the decade after the railway arrived. The foundation stone is dated 1890, and the simple brick church with its shingled bell turret was designed by Percy Monkton. In 1973 a very poor single-storeyed flat-roofed extension was built which obscures the nave. Behind the church is a 1990s church hall and a modern vicarage.

HORAM
The War Memorial c1960
H329062

Horam's war memorial, erected around 1920 and in the popular form of a Celtic wheel cross, was moved from this tranquil location to the churchyard of the parish church. Horam is famous for its Merrydown Cider factory. This started on a very small scale in 1949 in Jack Ward's garage, but he and Ian Howie were very successful; the present factory on the west side of Little London Road occupies the site of the manor house, which was gutted by fire after World War II. Merrydown is now an international company, and has diversified into wine.

HORAM, *The Brewers Arms, Vines Cross c1960*   H329093

A mile east of the village we reach the small hamlet of Vines Cross, which is centred on the former railway station site. Its name derives from John Vyne, a 16th-century vintner from nearby Hellingly. Still in the parish of Horam, Vines Cross is dominated by the Brewers Arms on the corner of Foordes Lane (right). In 1960 the pub was a tied house of Beard & Co of Lewes (the beer was soon after brewed for them by Harvey's of Lewes). The pub is now a Greene King house.

► **HORAM**

The Oast House c1960

H329070

A little north of Horam, on the Heathfield road and up Steelyards Hill, stands Stillyans, an oasthouse converted into a house. These tall conical tiled roofs are found all over Kent and Sussex in the hop growing regions. Hops were spread on sacking on a slatted first floor with a fire on the ground floor, and the hot air rose through the hops and vented through a cowl at the top. Many oast houses are now converted to houses - the oast itself makes interesting circular rooms.

◄ HORAM
Little London c1965
H329101

Parallel with and to the west of Steelyards Hill, the main A267 passes through the hamlet of Little London, a mile and a half north of Horam and still within its parish boundary. On the right, just out of view a little downhill, is a former Gospel Hall dated 1890 and now a house. The garage, Winter's Garage, has been modernised and has a high canopy over the modern petrol pumps. The cottages beyond of about 1900 remain, with the nearer one, Woodhay, extended.

◄ CROWBOROUGH
All Saints' Church 1900 44931

At the northernmost point away from Hailsham we reach Crowborough, a village that became a health resort in the 1870s when Lord Abergavenny followed the advice of a Dr Prince. On the eastern edge of the beautiful Ashdown Forest, the town is now a commuter settlement. On the north side of the village green, the church dates from 1744, including the tower and spire, with additions for Lord Abergavenny made in the 1880s. Beyond the Victorian lych gate is the vicarage, also of 1744.

69

▶ **EAST HOATHLY**
High Street c1965
E177042

From Crowborough the route heads back nearer to Hailsham's environs and to the village of East Hoathly, a village now much more peaceful than a few years ago. The road sign (left) at the junction of the High Street and London Road gives the clue. Fortunately for the village, it is now by-passed by the busy A22, but until then traffic had to negotiate this very sharp bend, and the London to Eastbourne traffic made the centre of the village a less than pleasant fume-filled place, I recall, particularly at weekends.

◀ **EAST HOATHLY**
High Street c1955
E177008r

The second view looks along Waldron Road into the High Street, with the London road turning beyond the houses on the right; the nearest of these, Warnham Cottage, is no longer a shop but a house. Beyond the Kings Head pub on the left, the white-painted shop has become a gift shop and café, and the large bay window to its far end is now demolished. The church-like brick building dates from 1900; it was built as a Sunday School, but has now lost its belfry turret.

▲ **EAST HOATHLY,** *The Church c1960* E177021

Hoathly is an Anglo-Saxon place name meaning 'heather-covered clearing'. It has a medieval parish church in the western part of the village, but all is not as it seems in this view from the east. Only the squat, battlemented tower is medieval, a 15th-century one paid for by the Pelham family of Halland. The rest is mostly an 1856 rebuild, with the flat-roofed vestry at the right added in 1901 and a lychgate (out of view to the left) in 1883. The churchyard is now trimmer, and much heather has been planted, possibly in honour of the village name.

◄ **CHIDDINGLY**
The Village c1955 C534005

South-east of East Hoathly lies the large scattered parish of Chiddingly, a typical rolling Wealden-edge village composed of scattered hamlets, farmsteads and woodland. The church is in one such hamlet with a pub, the Six Bells, nearby; this view looks uphill towards Church Lane at the crest. Beyond the building on the right, Yew Tree House with its yew tree, is the pub and church, the latter with its fine 130ft-high 15th-century spire and the Sir John Jefferay monument to the builder of Chiddingly Place (view C534004 on pages 72-73).

CHIDDINGLY
The Village and Place Farm c1955   C534004

We are looking in the opposite direction from view C534005 (page 71), downhill on a fine summer's day. There are estate cottages on the right, the ones in the foreground of the 1890s and the other pair dated 1874. The building on the left is Place Farm, formerly Chiddingly Place. This was a great Tudor mansion built by Sir John Jefferay, Baron of the Exchequer to Queen Elizabeth I. Much was demolished in the late 18th century, but one wing survived as a farmhouse, and another was converted into a barn. This important c1560 brick mansion is currently being restored to its former glory (January 2004).

▼ **CHIDDINGLY,** *Muddles Green c1955* C534008

Half a mile south of the hamlet with the parish church and Chiddingly Place is another small hamlet, Muddles Green, where cottages fringe a small green. All four buildings in this view are Victorian: the one on the left, Birch Cottage, is of the 1860s, and the one behind the telephone pole, Jubilee Cottage, is dated 1887, while the others are of about 1900. Behind the photographer is the 1906 village school, and on the right the green has been enlarged with new houses built in the 1990s, Willetts Field.

► **CHIDDINGLY**
Muddles Green c1955
C534011

Muddles Green gets its name from Nicholas Moodell of Waldron, who owned land here in the 16th century. Frith's photographer has now passed the primary school and is looking into the lane to Golden Cross. The conical roof on the left does not belong to a dovecote or fairytale castle but to a bungalow, and beyond is the roof of the old smithy cottage, now rebuilt as a bungalow. This view is taken from within the gate of the informal George V Jubilee Garden, presumably opened in 1935 or soon after.

◄ **UPPER DICKER**
The Downs c1955
U50009

Moving south to the Cuckmere River valley, our tour reaches Upper Dicker, about two and a half miles west of Hailsham. This curious name apparently comes from the Latin for a tenth or ten, the ten being iron rods or 'dickers' which a medieval ironmaster paid as his rent for the land hereabouts. This view looks south from the Michelham road towards the South Downs in the distance.

► **UPPER DICKER**
The Dicker c1955   U50018

This architecturally confused mansion is now part of St Bede's boarding school; it was previously the home of the notorious Horatio Bottomley MP. He married the owner of Weston's Cottage, a small cottage incorporated into his slowly built castle-cum-Swiss chalet confection – parts are dated 1908, but the house was begun in the 1890s. Bottomley got involved in selling titles and knighthoods; he crashed to earth in 1922 when he was jailed for fraud, dying in 1933 bankrupt and in poverty.

▶ **UPPER DICKER**
Stud Cottages
c1955 U50007

Bottomley did not pay his bills on time, and sometimes not at all, but he played the role of a genial squire with gusto; besides building estate cottages, he also bred race horses. He built Stud House for his trainer and this row of cottages for his stable lads and staff. Beyond are former stud buildings. All is now part of St Bede's School, with the cottages converted to dormitories and dormers added in the roof.

◀ **UPPER DICKER**
Coldharbour Road
c1955 U50015

This last view in Dicker looks towards the main crossroads and The Dicker, which is hidden by the distant trees. The left-hand trees surround the 1843 neo-Norman parish church of Holy Trinity. The openness on the right has now given way to modern houses, and the post office and general store on the left is now a private house. The late Victorian estate cottages in the distance are in a more picturesque Sussex tile-hung style with ornate bargeboards to their gables.

▶ **MICHELHAM PRIORY**
The Gatehouse c1965
M275007

Half a mile south-east of Dicker we reach Michelham Priory, the buildings set within a large rectangular wet moat fed by the Cuckmere River, which forms the moat's north-west arm. The 'island' formed by the moat is entered over a 16th-century bridge and through a fine 15th-century Wealden sandstone gatehouse, seen here from within the moat; the house is out of view to the right.

◀ **MICHELHAM PRIORY**
c1955 M275311

Michelham Priory was founded in 1229 as a house for thirteen Augustinian canons, who took over a Norman moated manor house. The priory was dissolved by Henry VIII in 1537 and the church was demolished, but much of the priory was incorporated in the Tudor mansion we see in this view from near the gatehouse. Medieval Gothic arches can be seen beyond the splendid cedar's spreading boughs, while the rest of the house has more of a Tudor character.

◄ **ARLINGTON**
The Cuckmere c1955
A347003

Two miles south-west of Michelham Priory, further downstream along the Cuckmere River, we reach Arlington, another scattered village of farmsteads bisected by the meandering river. The Cuckmere River rises six or so miles north-east of Hailsham and meanders past it to the west. Then it flows through the South Downs to reach the English Channel at Cuckmere Haven, where there is no port or settlement, unlike at Sussex's other river mouths such as the Arun, the Adur and the Ouse.

◄ MICHELHAM PRIORY
The Long Barn c1965
M275015

In 1959 Mrs Stella Hotblack bought the Priory and promptly gave it to the Sussex Archaeological Society, a pro-active antiquarian society that also owns Anne of Cleves House Museum in Lewes, Fishbourne Roman Palace and Lewes Castle. There are many attractions here, including a physic garden, a rope museum and an Iron Age centre. There are several important farm buildings, including the Long Barn, which has been dendro-chronologically dated to 1597-1601; the monks' watermill has been restored, and is now grinding corn again. This view shows the barn's steep roof and the later cart shed built alongside its main wall.

▲ **ARLINGTON,** *The Church c1955*   A347034

St Pancras' parish church is at the west of a small village situated on a low ridge above the Cuckmere River valley. An ancient church, it has an Anglo-Saxon nave with one small Roman brick-arched Saxon window intact high up to the right of the later porch. The squat 13th-century tower is unusual in that its oak-shingled spire starts well below the nave roof ridge. To the right beyond the trees is now a 2001 lychgate that leads into The Street, a short lane to the crossroads by the pub we see in view A347002, below.

◄ ARLINGTON
The Street c1960
A347002

From the churchyard The Street, a cul-de-sac, leads to the crossroads and the popular Yew Tree Inn, the building with the porch on the left, its Victorian brickwork now painted white. On the right we can see the timber-framed Tudor walls of The Corner House. In the distance is Tudor Cottage with its central chimney stack and steeply-pitched tiled roof, an early 16th-century timber-framed house now cased in brick.

BERWICK
Drusilla's Park,
The Shops c1955
B563049

From peaceful Arlington our route passes Arlington Reservoir before heading south to cross the A27 to Drusilla's Park, one of Sussex's major tourist attractions. These 1950s and 1960s views capture it as it was before more recent expansion. For several decades before this it had consisted of a cottage and converted outbuildings, with its principal attractions wallabies and a miniature railway. On the left is the Gift Shop, which still thrives.

▶ **BERWICK**
*Drusilla's Park,
the Thatched Tea Barn
c1965* B563051

Nowadays it is more of a proper zoo, with monkeys, flamingos, meerkats and all sorts of animals and birds, and with very much a stress on activities for children. Certainly my girls enjoyed their days out here with their grandparents. In the 1960s, cars parked amid the old buildings, and this view is taken from beside the vehicle entrance. Now there is a large car park further north, and pedestrians in the yard no longer have to compete with vehicles. The thatched barn is still a feature of the yard.

▶ **BERWICK**
*Drusilla's Park,
the Cottage c1955*
B563009

Fronting the road, beyond the outbuildings in the two previous views, is the 17th-century cottage where the zoo park started some seventy years ago; its outbuildings became the gift shop and tea rooms. The lane leads to Alfriston further down the Cuckmere River, a popular tourist village with its Clergy House. The ground floor of the cottage was used for tea rooms, but nowadays serves as the zoo offices.

◄ **BERWICK**
*Drusilla's Park,
the Old English
Tea Garden c1965*
B563047

This view was taken
behind the cottage in
View B563009 (page
82) – we can see the
old catslide tile roof of
the cottage on the
right sweeping down
to cover the lean-to.
In the 1960s the
cottage garden was
the Old English Tea
Garden. Out of view
to the right of the
camera is the gift
shop, and behind the
camera on the left is
the thatched tea room
we see in view
B563051 (page 82).

BERWICK
Drusilla's Park, the Miniature Railway c1955   B563014

The miniature railway was one of the major attractions of
Drusilla's and still is, though the engines are somehow less
utilitarian and more convincingly based on steam locomotives -
the best one is 'Ruston' The train now hauls visitors around
within the high-fenced zoo park.

WILMINGTON, *The Old Yew Tree c1960* W406006

From the modern, bustling entertainment of Drusilla's Zoo Park we finish this chapter in Wilmington, on the east side of the Cuckmere River. This very pretty village with its flint and brick houses and cottages runs south from the main road to its parish church of St Mary and St Peter, which is set high above the lane with the ruins of Wilmington Priory beyond. The chancel is Norman. To the north of the north porch there is a massive, very ancient yew tree, its weary boughs propped on posts. It is thought to be as old as the Norman church itself.

WILMINGTON
The Priory Ruins c1950 W406002

Immediately south of the church are the remains of Wilmington Priory. It was founded before 1100 by Robert of Mortain, William the Conqueror's half-brother, for the Benedictine monks of Grestain in Normandy - its abbey east of Honfleur is now also ruinous and a farmhouse. After the Dissolution it became a private house incorporating much of the priory buildings, and this view shows the south end of the 14th-century great hall with its flanking stair turrets and later Elizabethan window. Now owned by the Sussex Archaeological Society, as Michelham Priory is, it is still a private house, and the farm buildings we see here have been converted into dwellings.

WILMINGTON, *The Long Man c1965* W406008

A familiar sight for those heading to or from Eastbourne along the A27 as it passes north of the South Downs escarpment is the Long Man of Wilmington, a gigantic chalk figure of a man holding 250ft-long rods in each hand. The outline is now set out in white blocks installed in 1969. Although the first written reference to him is in the 18th century, his date is uncertain - some think he was created in the Bronze Age. This is a suitably enigmatic note upon which to end this second tour from Hailsham.

INDEX

NAMES OF SUBSCRIBERS

The following people have kindly supported this book by subscribing to copies before publication.

Mr B. S. & Mrs M. E. Adams, Hailsham

L. Allistone, Hailsham

Colin P. G. Angior, Heathfield

Bill & Frieda Applin, Hailsham

The Arndle Family, Herstmonceux

Mr R. J. & Mrs R. M. Attree, Hailsham

Mr & Mrs F. W. Bailey of Hailsham Radio

C. N. & P. P. Baker of Herstmonceux

The Bennett Family, Hailsham

Christine A. Brant

Mr K. C. & Mrs L. Briggs, Hailsham

Mr & Mrs Richard Brown, Hailsham

Bernadette Burton & Douglas Burton

Mr & Mrs A. J. Burton

R. W. & L. H. Butcher

In Memory of Mrs Ruby Carley, Hailsham

Jacqueline Charman & Trevor Charman

Marjorie Clarke

Mr R. J. & Mrs D. T. Colbran

Mr J. R. Crouch & Mrs S. M. Crouch

Mr A. Cripps & Mrs L. Cripps

In Memory of P. Cross, Hailsham

D. J. Cruse, Hailsham

J. A. J. Cruse, Hailsham

Elsie & Robert Cull

David, Marilyn & Victoria de Laney, Hailsham

Mrs Audrey Dibble, Hailsham

Mary Ellis, Hailsham

The Elsbury and Snoxell Families, Hailsham

Terry & Evelyn Evenden

Barbara Fletcher

Graeme Ford, Hailsham

Helene G. Ford, Hailsham

Paul Ford, Hailsham

Simon Ford, Hailsham

To my son, Michael Francis, Hailsham

Mr K. A. & Mrs S. E. French, Hailsham

Paul Funnell, Hailsham

Karen Furley, Hailsham

William A. George

Mr P. J. Girle & Mrs M. C. Girle of Hailsham

Robert Girling

Mrs Sophie Givan (nee Townsend)

Eileen Goad

Hailsham Gazette

Hazel & Edward Goad

Phil Goble (Green Bros) & son Clive

John K. Golding

Mr Gordon & Mrs Freda Head

Grangemead Resource Centre, Hailsham

Valerie T. Gray

The Gurr Family of Hailsham

Brian Darwin Haigh

Mr B. R. Hanks, Herstmonceux

Mr R. & Mrs J. Hayward-Lynch, Hailsham

Alan Hillman and Family, Hailsham

Bill & Connie Hilton and Family, Hailsham

Mr P. & Mrs J. Hobden, Hailsham

In Memory of George & Florrie Horn

John Humphries, Hailsham

Rev. Alan W. Hunt & Mrs Ann Hunt

To my son Grahame Jones, Hailsham

To Ken with love from Mag

The King Family, Ravenscourt

The Kirk Family, Hailsham

Kay Langridge

To Janet Large, love Peg & Denis

J. & R. Larkin, Hailsham

Mrs Maureen Leek, Hailsham

Ken Lock

Mary E. Lown

Jill Lucas of Hailsham

Peter & Jennie Mansfield

Mr Doug Martin

Mr D. A. & Mrs P. J. Martin, Hailsham

Irene Mauldon (Sands)

E. Moore

Keith Mullen

In Memory of Laurie Mynett, Hailsham

S. G. Newnham

David Alan Nicholson

The Page Family, Hailsham

Barry Pannett

Ian Parks

Personal Service Travel

'In Memory of a Happy Childhood',
D. Phillips

Michael J. Powell, Hailsham

Margaret & Roger Pye

Shirley & Henry Roberts of Hailsham

Ray & Nora Roberts, Hailsham, East Sussex

Susan Robertson

Mark Ryland

Mr J. H. Salter & Mrs M. P. Salter

Michael & Linda Sanders, Hailsham

Mr A. G. Saunders & Mrs B. J. Saunders

Peg & Denis Simmons

Ths Skilton Family, Hailsham

The Smith Family, Hailsham

Mr J. C. & Mrs S. M. Smith, Hailsham

Maureen Spring & Ted Spring

The Stevens Family, Hailsham, Sussex

Christopher J. Stoakley, Hailsham

Mr A. & Mrs J. Sumner and Family, Hailsham

Sussex Express

George Henry Sykes

Don Taylor Plumbing & Heating Services
1933-1971

John & Bonnie Taylor and Family of Hailsham

Daniel G. Terry

Mr & Mrs Thexton

To Dr Robert Thornton

To Morris Thornton

Paul & Daren Thorpe

Roland & Pauline Thorpe (nee Horn)

The Tilleard Family, Hailsham 2004

P. J. C. & A. J. Tuppen

Valerie & Trevor Vincent

Adrian Wainwright

Tom Walter

Mr J. R. Walter & Mrs V. F. Walter, Hailsham

Mr & Mrs Webber

Mr A. D. Webbon

Mr M. J. & Mrs C. M. Webster-Jones

Mr M. J. & Mrs S. Wells, Hailsham

Violet & Colin Whistler, Hailsham

Catherine & Brian Wicks, Hailsham

Mrs Naomi Wilson

Carol Wood

R. Wright

Barbara Young (nee Jarvis)

FREE MOUNTED PRINT

Mounted Print
Overall size 14 x 11 inches

Fill in and cut out this voucher and return
it with your remittance for £2.25 (to cover postage and handling). Offer valid for delivery to UK addresses only.

Choose any photograph included in this book.
Your SEPIA print will be A4 in size. It will be mounted in a cream mount with a burgundy rule line (overall size 14 x 11 inches).

**Order additional Mounted Prints
at HALF PRICE (only £7.49 each*)**
If you would like to order more Frith prints from this book, possibly as gifts for friends and family, you can buy them at half price (with no additional postage and handling costs).

Have your Mounted Prints framed
For an extra £14.95 per print* you can have your mounted print(s) framed in an elegant polished wood and gilt moulding, overall size 16 x 13 inches (no additional postage and handling required).

---

* IMPORTANT!

These special prices are only available if you order at the same time as you order your free mounted print. You must use the ORIGINAL VOUCHER on this page (no copies permitted). We can only despatch to one address.

Send completed Voucher form to:
The Francis Frith Collection, Frith's Barn, Teffont, Salisbury, Wiltshire SP3 5QP